About the Author

Mzee (m-zay) Marula is the pen name of Richard L. Howell who lives and writes in America but whose heart is always in the African bush.

Special thanks to C.E. Latham

Dedication

This book is dedicated to the conservation of the animals and people of the African bush in honor of the Creator who made them.

Farkin Publications is proud to introduce Professor Meerkat® Volume One of "African Animals A,B,C,'s. This colorfully illustrated book introduces children ages 5 through 12 to the 'See and Say' method of vocabulary and language building for English using phonics.

If you wish to participate in sending this book to children in Africa or other countries you may purchase copies of it on Amazon or through Farkin Publications at <u>farkinpublications@netzero.net</u>

Please direct inquiries and comments to
<u>farkinpublications@netzero.net</u>

Welcome to Professor Meerkat's® *African Animals ABC's See and Say* ©.

The purpose of this book is to promote English literacy among children around the world and to raise awareness of the precious animals that Creator has made for our wonder, enjoyment and care.

Our motto is "No more extinct animals."

We hope you enjoy reading, teaching and sharing this book with your students, friends and family.

"Creator has made the world knowable and worth knowing about."

Mzee Marula

For God so loved the world that He gave His only begotten Son, that whosoever believeth in Him should not perish, but have everlasting life. John 3:16

Farkin Publications LLC

Fort Worth, Texas

Teacher's Guide:

This book is created to be used with the Phonetic Method of teaching vocabulary and reading. It is suggested that the teacher read the factoid and the prose and then have the class repeat part or all of the factoid and prose.

Depending on age and time factors, encourage discussion of the factoid and prose, using the illustration to reinforce repetition of the letters of the alphabet, and relating the meaning of the prose through the factoid and illustration, adjusted to the age of the class.

Above all enjoy the experience and thank you for the wonderful work only you can do as a teacher.

Mzee Marula

African Animals ABC's

Factoids: African Aardvark
Did you know?

- medium-sized, burrowing, nocturnal mammal native to Africa.
- uses it's long snout to sniff out food
- roams over most of the southern two-thirds of the African plain
- eats ants and termites, ears like a rabbit
- dig burrows in the ground where they live
- it's closest living relative could be the elephant
- called the "Ant-bear"

Aa: Annie and Andy
The African Aardvark

Annie and Andy the African aardvark
Went for a walk after dark.
They came upon a termite mound,
Which we know, holds their favorite food.
As they began to eat their favorite treat,
a leopard they did meet.

"We're Antbears" said Annie.
"Yes, we sure are" said Andy.
"Well I guess I'll just go,"the leopard said,
"You would be no treat for me to eat."

African Animals ABC's

Factoids: African Baboon
Did you know?

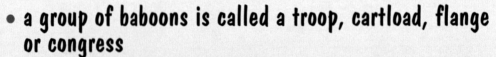

- a group of baboons is called a troop, cartload, flange or congress
- communicate using 30 different ways which include screams, grunts and barks
- female baboon is half the size of the male
- live in grassland, rocky desert and rainforest
- do not have tails to grip with so they spend more time on the ground
- are aggressive and harm domestic animals and people
- Baboons actually dance by the light of the full moon when they are with their troop

Bb: Betty and Billy
    The African Baboon

Betty and Billy the African Baboon
Danced and danced all night
By the light of the full moon.
But when the sun came up,
They finally gave up and slept until late afternoon.

Betty and Billy the African Baboon
Danced by the light of the summer moon,
They danced all night until daylight
And slept until late afternoon.

African Animals ABC's

Factoids: African Cheetah
Did you know?

- fastest land animal can run up to 70mph or 110kph
- claws work like cleats on a football shoe providing lots of traction when running
- most endangered African cat, only 10,000 left
- has no fear because he can outrun anything
- make docile pets
- elegant and beautiful
- uses tail for balance

Cc: Chelsie and Charlie
The African Cheetah

Charlie the African Cheetah
Said to Chelsea the African Cheetah
As they lay under a tree one day
"I'm not afraid of any animal on the plain!"
"Well, neither am I" said Chelsea to Charlie
"I'm not afraid of anything!"
"Oh, you brag so much"
Said Chelsea to Charlie.

"Well, said Charlie to Chelsea "Do you know why?"
"Yes of course, silly boy all Cheetahs know why;
It's because we're the fastest animal
on the African plain
and we can outrun anything! "

African Animals ABC's

Factoids: African Duiker
Did you know?

- small, agile with slender legs, wedge-shaped heads topped by a crest of long hair and relatively large eyes
- horns are small and spike-like lying flat against the head
- freeze and crouch when danger is near to escape detection
- when disturbed they plunge into thick brush to hide. This trait is the source of their name "Duiker" which in Dutch means "diver".
- the young utter a loud bleat when in danger, quickly signaling adults in the area
- courtship involves prolonged and noisy chases about the territory before mating

Dd: Debbie and Danny
The African Duiker

Danny the African duiker
loved Debbie the African duiker,
And he never went anywhere without her.
He would run and run
Just to show her he liked her.
Neither lion nor leopard
Did they fear
And if one came near
They would dive into the brush,
And Debbie would say "shush"
And Danny would smile
And whisper, "Yes, dear!"

African Animals ABC's

Factoids: African Elephant
Did you know?

- trunk is about seven feet (two meters) long
- use their trunk as snorkel when they wade in deep water
- use their trunk to spray water on themselves, usually followed by a layer of dirt for a protective barrier
- trunk can perform delicate maneuvers such as picking a berry from the ground or plucking a single leaf off a tree
- if threatened, uses its trunk to make loud trumpeting noises as a warning
- sometimes hug by wrapping their trunks together in displays of greeting and affection
- just as a human baby sucks its thumb, an elephant calf often sucks its trunk for comfort

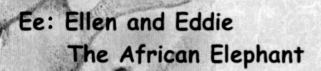

Ee: Ellen and Eddie
The African Elephant

Ellen and her baby, Eddie,
Went down to the river,
Which was Eddie's favorite place to play.
"You need a bath," said Ellen.
But Eddie said "Not today."
"Yes, and then you can play."
So she filled up her trunk
And gave him a dunk,
And he played the rest of the day.

African Animals ABC's

Factoids: African Bat-Eared Fox
Did you know?

- their teeth are small and they have up to 8 extra molars to grind the hard casings of the insects which they eat, mainly termites
- both parents take part in rearing their young
- distinguishable by their huge ears and ark eye mask
- their huge ears (both external and internal) are designed to detect even the tiniest insects moving around.
- using their highly sensitive bat-like ears they can even detect beetle larvae that are a foot underground

Ff: Fanny and Freddie
The African Bat-Eared Fox

Fanny and Freddie the African bat-eared fox
Were playing one day,
When a huge termite mound
They found on their way.
"What a delicious snack" said Freddie to Fannie.
"There's more than enough for both you and me."
"Yes", said Fannie to Freddie,
With my big ears
I hear more than a few.
Plenty for both me and you."

"You're right I can hear too,
But exactly how many
I really can't tell."
So they ate and ate
This tasty treat
And both were right,
There were more than both could eat!

African Animals ABC's

Factoids: African Giraffe
Did you know?

- their long tongues are helpful in eating because they help pull leaves from the trees
- spending most of the day eating, a full-grown giraffe consumes 45kg (100 pounds) of leaves and twigs a day
- the male giraffe is both taller and heavier than the female
- both sexes have skin-covered knobs, called ossicones on the top of their heads
- female ossicones are smaller and have a small tuft of fur on top, while male ossicones are bald on the top.
- Giraffes sleep less than two hours a day, they usually sleep with their feet tucked under them and their head resting on their hindquarters

Gf: Gina and George
The African Giraffes

Gina and George the African Giraffes
Were munching on tree leaves
With their long black tongues one day
when George heard Gina say
"I'm as tall as a tree"
You're right said George, but not as tall as me"
"You can run faster than me", said he to she.

"That's true and I'm also smarter than you." said she to he.
Then stuck out her tongue
And laughed as they both
Ran along.

14

African Animals ABC's

Factoids: African Hippopotumus
Did you know?

- the hippo's nose, ears, and eyes are on the top of its head, and they protrude from the water while the rest of its head and its body lie beneath the surface
- they can walk along the bottoms of rivers and lakes
- are excellent swimmers and can hold their breath for about five minutes
- at dusk will walk as far as 5 miles to graze until dawn
- may eat up to 150 pounds (68 kilograms) of grass a night

Hh: Haley and Harry
African Hippopotumus

Haley and Harry African Hippos
Were standing by the river one moonlit night.
"My what a beautiful sight!"
Said Haley to Harry.
"Yes dear, I quite agree,
Care to take a stroll with me?"
"Sure my dear", said he to she.
"By the river or on the bottom,
"Which shall it be?"
"With the moon to light our way the bottom"
He heard her say.
They didn't need to talk
on this underwater walk!

African Animals ABC's

Factoids: African Impala
Did you know?

- they are fast runners who can leap up to 10m in length and 3m in height
- they use their tremendous speed and agility to avoid predators and seemingly for pure enjoyment
- most young impala are born around mid-day as this is the safest time to give birth since most of their enemies (lions etc..) are resting
- the name 'Impala' comes from the Zulu language meaning 'gazelle'
- they can release a scent from glands on their heels which can help them stay together, this is done by performing a high kick of their hind legs

Ii: Ida and Iggy
The African Impala

Ida and Iggy the African Impala
Ran and ran, and jumped and jumped,
And played and played all day.
"I have two names"
Said Ida the African Impala
To Iggy the African Impala.
"My Zulu name is gazelle,
But please don't tell."

"Why not?" said Iggy the African Impala
To Ida the African Impala,
"Because someone might laugh at me!"
"Oh, that's ok" said Iggy to Ida,
"It would only be because of jealousy,
When they see you can run as fast as me!"

African Animals ABC's

Factoids: African Jackal
Did you know?

- have doglike features and a bushy tail
- male and female mate for life
- yipping calls are made when the family gathers
- a pair of jackals will move through their territory at a fast trot, stopping frequently to examine something, sniff the air or listen; ready for any opportunity that might provide a meal
- Eagles are small pups biggest threat

Jj: Jessie an Jimmy
The African Jackal

"Yip, yip,yip" said Jessie the African Jackal
To Jimmy the African Jackal
And the rest of her family.
"Come run and play with me."
"We're hungry right now
Too busy to play,
We haven't found a thing to eat all day!"

"Okay, okay", said Jessie.
"Run over this way,
And you all will be full
For the rest of this day.
But be careful as you run;
While you're having fun,
Remember your pups are
An eagles favorite treat to eat!"

African Animals ABC's

Factoids: African Kudu
Did you know?

- are capable of jumping as high as 7 feet
- males often have spiral horns with almost 2 or 2 1/2 beautiful twists while females don't have horns at all
- males are double the size of females
- male kudos show their dominance by standing next to another and the one with the larger body is considered the leader
- these antelope produce loud sounds in the form of a gruff bark
- Kudus are known as "The Ghost of Africa"

Kk: Katy and Kevin
The African Kudu

Katy the African Kudu
Said to Kevin the African Kudu
"Why am I not as big as you?
Why do you have horns and not me too?
Why do we bark instead of growl?
Why, why, why?"
"Indeed", said Kevin the African Kudu to Katy in reply.
"Creator made me big and you small
Because that is best and that is all."

African Animals ABC's

Factoids: African Lion
Did you know?

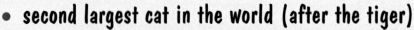

- second largest cat in the world (after the tiger)
- a group of lions is called a "pride"
- the male's thick manes protect their necks when they fight with challengers
- females are the primary hunters and work as a team to take down prey.
- after a successful hunt, all the lions in the pride share the meal. But there is a pecking order with the adult males taking first claim followed by the lionessess, and finally, the cubs
- spend up to 16-20 hours of the day sleeping or resting, they can be found lying on their backs with their feet up or taking a snooze in a tree
- while lazing around, they are very affectionate towards one another, rubbing heads, grooming and purring

Ll: Lilly and Larry
The African Lion

Larry the African Lion
Said to Lilly the African Lion
"Only the Tiger is bigger than me!
But I am still King of the jungle don't you see!"
"Ha!", said Lilly to Larry in reply,
"All I see is a lazy lion in a tree!"
Then she purred affectionately,
"You are my king, that is true,
For none are as brave or handsome as you!"
Larry smiled as he roared, and thought, "How nice it is to be adored!"

African Animals ABC's

Factoids: African Meerkat
Did you know?

- live in the Kalahari desert
- a group is called a "mob" or "gang"
- has dark bands around eyes and a white face
- while the others are eating one will stand watch against predators
- stands on rocks or in bushes when keeping lookout against predators
- is very sociable and lives with up to 30 other meerkats in underground burrows

Mm: Mr. and Mrs. Meerkat
The African Meerkat

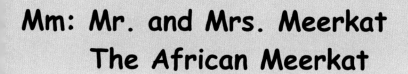

Mr. Meerkat the African Meerkat
Married Mary Meerkat
And that was that.
She would cook
And he would look
While all the little Meerkats ran and played.
Too short to see most everything,
Unless he rose on his toes or was a jumping.
So jump, jump, jump
Up on your toes
And look real good
Or else your family will be
Someone else's food!

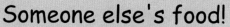

African Animals ABC's

Factoids: African Nyala
Did you know?

- hairier version of the sitatunga and is only found in the southeastern parts of Africa
- adult males and females look vastly different. Males are slate grey to dark brown with up to 14 distinct white stripes across the back going down to the flanks. Has white stripes on its thighs and bellies, the bottom of their legs are yellow and have a mane of long white hair running down to the tail.
- females have a bright chestnut color with up to 18 stripes across their back and flanks and do not have manes or fringes of long hair
- will often associate with troops of monkeys and baboons to take advantage of fallen fruit

Nn: Nellie and Nigel
The African Nyala

Nellie and Nigel the African Nyala
Were eating their favorite fruit
With a family of monkeys
and baboons in a troop.
Nellie the African Nyala
Said to Nigel the African Nyala,
"Wow, we have quite a group,
I hope there will be enough for all to eat.
Monkeys see and monkeys do, and baboons too!

While we eat they pick and play
with the fruit we found today.
Then we watch while they eat away
It just seems best that way.
We are all safe and there's enough,
To make sure we are all stuffed!"

African Animals ABC's

Factoids: African Ostritch
Did you know?

- the tallest and heaviest of all birds
- can run just over 40 miles an hour (64 kph) for a short distance and keep up a speed of more than 30 mph (48 kph) over longer distances
- uses its short wings for balance, holding them outstretched when it runs
- has very strong legs which can also be used for self-defense
- can kick with the force strong enough to kill a lion
- when danger approaches, an ostritch will often lie low to hide, stretching its neck along the ground, its feather colors blend with the sandy soil where it lives. From far away, it looks like the ostrich has buried its head in the sand

Oo: Olivia and Ollie
The African Ostrich

Olivia the African Ostrich
Said to Ollie the African Ostrich
"We are the tallest and heaviest
Of all the birds.
Are we really birds since we can't fly?"
"Well Creator made us
This way so they say.
Why we can run almost all day
Especially when danger comes
And we have to get away.
Sometimes we just lie low to hide,
With our necks outstretched

And feathers from our wings to the side
With a kick so strong
We can kill a lion,
So as we are we are just fine.
No more talk about what we can't do,
Just be thankful for what we can!"

African Animals ABC's

Factoids: African Porcupine
Did you know?

- lives south of the Sahara to South Africa
- live in deep burrows in the ground
- sleep during the day and search for food at night
- warns predators by grunting, stamping feet and spreading its long sharp quills
- its quills are easily detached from its body and embedded in a predator when attacked

Pp: Patty and Paulie
The African Porcupine

Patty and Paulie the African Porcupine
Were playing in the sand one day.
"You're a pig!" said Patty the African Porcupine
To Paulie the African Porcupine
As he kicked sand at her just for play."
"Oh no I'm not"He said in reply.
"Then don't treat me that way!"
"Well some call us quill pigs
And that's a fact
Even though we're rodents
More like the rat."
"I am sorry", said Paulie the
African Porcupine,"for what I did"
"And I am sorry for what I said",
Pattie replied as she cried.
"Please don't cry my dearest dear,
All I want is you near.
When danger comes we will shake our quills
And together we will face all fears.
You're beautiful in black and white
Both in the day and at night.
Creator made us just right!"

African Animals ABC's

Factoids: African Quagga
Did you know?

- is a subspecies of the zebra
- is extinct
- looks like a cross between wild horses (rear end) and a zebra (head and neck, brown in color)
- went extinct around 1883, most likely due to excessive hunting by humans
- named for the sound of the warning call it makes which sounded like "kwa-ha-ha"

Qq: Queenie and Quinn
The African Quagga

"Quagga? Quagga?" said Queenie the African Quagga
To Quinn the African Quagga,
What's a Quagga?"
"You mean who's a Quagga don't you?", said Quinn to Queenie.
"Oh you know what I mean, don't you?
We are supposed to be extinct,
But here am I and there are you,
both Quagga two by two."
"Well, said Queenie, look at you,
Half a zebra in front of you
And half a horse behind you, ha, ha, ha!"
"Well, so are you and so pretty too.
Why thank you dear for making it clear!"

African Animals ABC's

Factoids: African Rhinoceros
Did you know?

- inspite of being large and bulky the rhino is very agile and can turn quickly in a small space
- the name rhinoceros means "nose horn"
- it is the second largest land animal, elephant being the largest
- can grow over 6 feet tall and over 11 feet long
- has thick skin which is sensitive to sunburns and insect bites, so they wallow in mud to create a protective barrier
- horns are made from keratin (basically compacted hair)
- can run up to 30 to 40 miles per hour (48kph to 64kph)
- has poor eyesight but a good sense of smell and hearing

Rr: Rhonda and Randy
The African Rhinoceros

Rhonda the African Rhinoceros
Said to Randy the African Rhinoceros
While strolling down a trail one day,
"Don't you think it's rather preposterous
This being a Rhinoceros with the nose horn and all?

"Think of all we have
And then you'll find it's not so bad", said Randy.
"Well perhaps you're right," said she to he.
"Let's see! Bigger than most
Except for the Elephant;
Faster than most even though we are so big", said Rhonda.
"Very true," said Randy,
"But most of all
Is how beautiful you are to me!"

African Animals ABC's

Factoids: African Sitatunga
Did you know?

- most aquatic (living in or around water) of all antelope species
- live in deeps swamps, wetlands, and forest areas near lake and river systems
- Sitatunga coats are shaggy and several inches long. Their thin hair is also coated with an oily, water-repellent secretion.
- hooves are often described as banana-like because they are elongated and will splay widely apart to keep them from sinking into soif soil
- the Sitatunga's hooves make them awkward and clumsy on the ground but allow them to stand and walk on floating islands of vegatation in the swamp
- are excellent swimmers

Ss: Sally and Sammy
The African Sitatunga

Sally the African Sitatunga
Said to Sammy the African Sitatunga
While swimming in the river one day.
"Sammy, some might laugh and say
When you walk upon the ground
You're near to falling down,
But when I see you in the water
You are graceful as an otter!"

"Thank you dear
For seeing me so clear
And not laughing like the others!"

African Animals ABC's

Factoids: African Topi
Did you know?

- among the fastest of antelopes reaching a speed of up to 70 miles per hour (112 kph) when being chased by a predator
- the Maasai describe them as wearing a suede jacket, blue jeans and yellow boots
- medium sized antelope with a striking reddish-brown to purplish-red coat that is glossy
- live in herds of 15-20 usually
- Topi eat only grass
- both male and female Topis like to rub their heads on the ground (to spread scent from their facial glands), roll in earth and stir up mud with their horns. They smear mud on their bodies with their hooves

Tt: Tina and Timmy
The African Topi

Timmy the African Topi
Loved to chase Tina the African Topi
Until one day to Timothy she did say,
"Why are you always chasing me that way?
I just wish you would go away!"
"It's only because I love you
And want to marry you some day", she heard him say.
"Well in that case, it's quite different, you may chase away!!"

African Animals ABC's

Factoids: African Unstriped Ground Squirrel

Did you know?

- families and communities all live together in burrows and colonies in and around parts of Africa
- are pretty much vegetarians and love to eat roots, seeds, fruit, pods, grains, insects, bird eggs and small animals
- they can grow to a length of 10-12 inches long (25-30cm) are sometimes kept as pets
- the young babies are called 'pup, kit, or kitten'. Females are called 'doe' and males are called 'buck'. A group of unstriped ground squirrels are called a 'dray or scurry'.
- they mostly live in the dry savanna and shrubland of Africa

Uu: Uma and Uni
The African Unstriped Ground Squirrel

Uma the African Unstriped Ground Squirrel
Asked Uni the African Unstriped Ground
As they munched on birds eggs
They had found that day,
Why do they call you buck
And call me doe
And call our kids kittens as they say?"

"Well, I don't know", Said Uni to Uma
As they walked along that day,
It just seems it's always been that way,
It's really hard to say!"

African Animals ABC's

Factoids: African Vulture
Did you know?

- huge species
- 37-45 inches (90cm-114cm) in body length, and wingspan of 8.2-9.5 feet (2.4m-2.9m)
- blackish coloring on top surface of body with a strongly contrasting white thigh feathers. Its black feathers on the back are lined with brown the vultures underside can range from pure white to buff-brown
- has a bald head with coloration that can range from reddish to dull pink
- is a scavenging bird, feeding mostly on dead animals which it finds by site from the air or other vultures
- generally solitary animals
- keen eyesight

Vv: Veronica and Vinnie
The African Vulture

Fly, fly, fly!
Higher and higher they went,
High above the African plain.
Veronica the African Vulture
Said to Vinnie the African Vulture,

"I am so thankful
Creator made us this way,
Because I just love to fly
And soar all day!"

"Me too", said Vinnie
As he flew on his way.
"Without these big wings
There would be no way!"

African Animals ABC's

Factoids: African Wildebeest
Did you know?

- belong to the antelope family
- although large and stocky they are fast and agile when running
- there are two species of wildebeest, blue and black. The differences are horn curving and color of fur
- they live in the African plains and open woodlands
- they have migration periods throughout the year that they follow for food and water
- they are very vulnerable to large cats such as lions and other predators so they travel in herds
- they also stay close to zebras that are also prey to large predators when the alarm is sounded by a zebra the wildebeest know to flee

Ww: Winnie and Walter
The African Wildebeest

"Why oh why?"
Said Winnie the African Wildebeest
To Walter the African Wildebeest
"Do some live and some die?"
"It's just part of life
I don't really know why", Walter did reply.
"Well" said Winnie to Walter,
"I 'll bet there's a reason
Even if I don't know why."
"Of course there is,
Because Adam made the world that way and that is why!"

46

African Animals ABC's

Factoids: African X Mystery Animal Did you know?

- there are 16,938 identified endangered species of African animals and 10,000 birds which are endangered
- top 10 endangered species are:
  1. Elephant
  2. Penguin
  3. Lion
  4. Cheetah
  5. Black Rhino
  6. Addax
  7. Ethiopian Wolf
  8. Mountain Gorilla
  9. Pigmy Hippo
  10. Wild Dog

- We do not know our mystery animal because it is extinct.
- We must all work together to protect and conserve the wonderful creatures that Creator has made for us all to enjoy. Thank you,

  Professor Meerkat

African Animals ABC's Review

Aa - Aardvark

Bb - Baboon

Cc - Cheetah

Dd - Duiker

Ee - Elephant

Ff - Bat-eared Fox

Gg - Giraffe

Hh - Hippopotamus

Ii - Impala

Jj - Jackal

Kk - Kudu

Ll - Lion

Mm - Meerkat

Nn - Nyala

Oo - Ostrich

Pp - Porcupine

Qq - Quagga

Rr - Rhinoceros

Ss - Sitatunga

Tt - Topi

Uu - Unstriped Ground Squirrel

Vv - Vulture

Ww - Wildebeest

Xx - Mystery Animal

Yy - Yellow Billed Hornbill

Zz - Zebra

19 Because that which may be known about God is revealed in them;
for God has showed *it* to them.
20 For the invisible things of Him from the creation of the world
are clearly seen, being understood by the things that are made,
even his eternal power and Godhead; so that they are without excuse -
Romans 1:19-20

African Animals ABC's

Factoids: African Yellowbilled Hornbill
Did you know?

- live in dry and semi-arid areas of Sub-Saharan Africa
- eat fruit, seeds, leaves, insects, small mammals, lizards and snakes
- threats are crowned eagles, leopards, chimpanzees, and humans
- they nest in holes in trees
- they have a long down curved beak that can look like and turned down banana
- their heavy bill helps with cracking nuts, fighting and preening
  they travel in pairs or small family groups

Yy: Yari and Yulli the African Yellowbilled Hornbill

"What a preposterous proboscis Creator has given both of us",
Said Yari the African Yellowbilled Hornbill to Yulli the African Yellowbilled Hornbill.
"Well at least we don't look as monstrous as a Rhinoceros", said Yulli.
"Besides Creator never makes a mistake in whatever He makes."
"You're right"she replied,"and besides, how could we do our jobs in eating things
With hard shells or even enjoy so many different smells without these noses."
"That's right", he said "and we would just squawk instead of talk."
"If we could not talk I would be sad and so now you've helped me understand I am oh so glad."
"Well it looks like I have a banana in my mouth", said Yulli.
"Well, you look really cute with a banana for a snoot!" Yuri smiled and said.

50

African Animals ABC's

Factoids: African Zebra
Did you know?

- each has its own unique pattern of stripes
- they stick together and travel in large herds when migrating to better grasslands
- within a herd zebras stick to smaller family groups (males, females, offspring
- their teeth keep growing for the entire life as constant grazing wears them down
- might travel in mixed herds with other grazers such as wildebeests
- they are under constant threat of large predators

Zz: Zadie and Zach the African Zebra

Zadie the African Zebra said to Zach the African Zebra
as they ran and jumped and neighed,
"Yipes,stripes look how many of us Creator has made!
Little ones, big ones and we all look the same!"
"Oh no", said Zach answering back,
"Not a single one of us are the same
Except perhaps in name!"
"We may all be called Zebra,
That's our name but we each are different
Like raindrops on the plain!"

Made in the USA
Middletown, DE
27 October 2022

13547838R00033